Maths at Work

Maths at the Airport

Tracey Steffora

Raintree is an imprint of Capstone Global Library Limited, a company incorporated in England and Wales having its registered office at 7 Pilgrim Street, London, EC4V 6LB – Registered company number: 6695582

www.raintreepublishers.co.uk
myorders@raintreepublishers.co.uk

Text © Capstone Global Library Limited 2013
First published in hardback in 2013
Paperback edition first published in 2014
The moral rights of the proprietor have been asserted.

Edited by Dan Nunn and Abby Colich
Designed by Victoria Allen
Picture research by Tracy Cummins
Production control by Victoria Fitzgerald
Printed and bound in China by Leo Paper Products Ltd

ISBN 978 1 406 25071 8 (hardback)
16 15 14 13 12
10 9 8 7 6 5 4 3 2 1

ISBN 978 1 406 25078 7 (paperback)
17 16 15 14 13
10 9 8 7 6 5 4 3 2 1

British Library Cataloguing in Publication Data
Steffora, Tracey.
Maths at the airport. – (Maths at work)
510-dc23
A full catalogue record for this book is available from the British Library.

Acknowledgements
We would like to thank the following for permission to reproduce photographs: Alamy: p. 14 (© Jim West); Corbis: pp. 15 (© Robert Maass); dreamstime: p. 21 (Fintastique); Getty Images: pp. 6 (Jupiterimages), 9 (Lester Lefkowitz), 10 (Digital Vision), 11 (Andreas Koerner), 16 (Thinkstock), 18 (Karen Moskowitz), 23a (Jupiterimages); iStockphoto: pp. 5 (© Gene Chutka), 12 (© bojan fatur), 17 (© Gene Chutka), 19 (© mayo5); Shutterstock: pp. 4 (yxm2008), 7 (Remzi), 8 (Lisa S.), 13 (Lars Christensen), 20 (Eric Gevaert), 23b (Eric Gevaert).

Front cover photograph of a pilot sitting at the controls of a commercial aeroplane reproduced with permission from Getty Images/ Digital Vision/ James Lauritz.

Back cover photograph of a ground controller on a runway reproduced with permission from iStockphoto (© mayo5).

The publishers would like to thank Andy Colich for his invaluable help in the preparation of this book.

Every effort has been made to contact copyright holders of any material reproduced in this book. Any omissions will be rectified in subsequent printings if notice is given to the publisher.

Contents

Maths at the airport

Many people work at the airport.

Many people use maths at
the airport.

Counting

flight attendant

The flight attendant counts tickets.

The flight attendant
counts passengers.

baggage handler

The baggage handler counts bags.

How many bags can you count?

(answer on page 22)

9

Measuring

pilot

The pilot flies the plane.

The pilot measures how fast the plane is flying.

how high

The pilot measures how high the plane is flying.

plane

tree

Which is higher? The plane or the tree? (answer on page 22)

Shape and size

The screener looks at bags.

X-ray

The screener looks at the shape
of things inside the bags.

Some bags are large. The flight
attendant puts these bags in
(16) a locker.

Smaller bags go under the seat.

Is this bag large or small?

(answer on page 22)

Time

ground controller

The ground controller tells a plane when to move.

ground controller

The ground controller tells a plane
when to stop.

The air controller tells a plane when to fly.

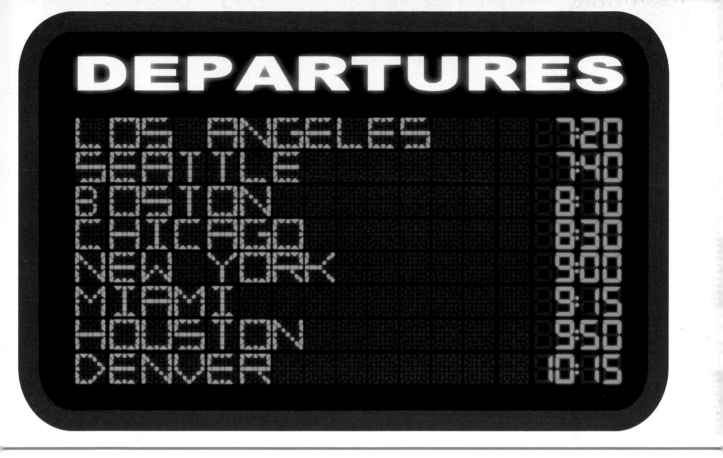

DEPARTURES

LOS ANGELES	7:20
SEATTLE	7:40
BOSTON	8:10
CHICAGO	8:30
NEW YORK	9:00
MIAMI	9:15
HOUSTON	9:50
DENVER	10:15

What time does the plane fly to
New York? (answer on page 22)

Answers

page 9: There are five bags.

page 13: The plane is higher than the tree.

page 17: The bag is small.

page 21: The plane flies to New York at 9.00.